Patterson Elementary School
3731 Lawrence Drive
Naperville, IL 60564

Bones and Muscles

Angela Royston

SEA-TO-SEA
Mankato Collingwood London

This edition first published in 2011 by
Sea-to-Sea Publications
Distributed by Black Rabbit Books
P.O. Box 3263, Mankato, Minnesota 56002

Printed in China, Dongguan

Library of Congress Cataloging-in-Publication Data

Royston, Angela.
Bones and muscles / Angela Royston.
p. cm. -- (Your body. Inside and out)
Includes index.
ISBN 978-1-59771-263-7 (library binding)
1. Musculoskeletal system--Juvenile literature. I. Title.
QP301.R694 2011
612.7--dc22
2010003823

9 8 7 6 5 4 3 2

Published by arrangement with the
Watts Publishing Group Ltd., London.

Series editor: Sarah Peutrill
Art director: Jonathan Hair
Design: Mo Choy
Consultant: Peter Riley
Photographer: Paul Bricknell
Illustrations: Ian Thompson

Picture credits: Peter Adams/zefa/Corbis: 17. H. Benser/zefa/Corbis: 28b.
Dept. of Clinical Radiology, Salisbury District Hospital/SPL: 28t. Laureen
Morgane/zefa/Corbis: 24. David Raymer/Corbis: 20. Paul A. Souders/Corbis:
15. Hattie Young/SPL: 29t.

Every attempt has been made to clear copyright.
Should there be any inadvertent omission please apply
to the publisher for rectification.

March 2010
RD/6000006414/002

Contents

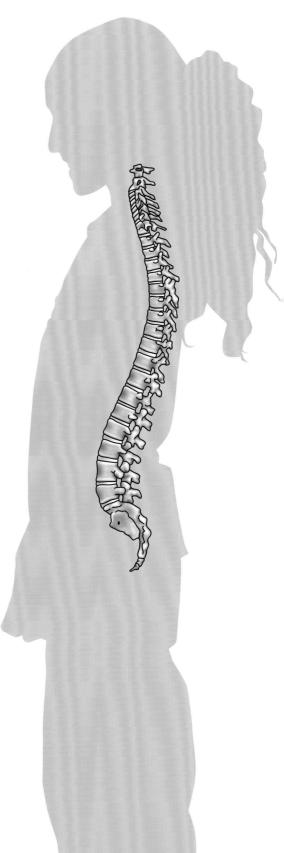

Under Your Skin

You can move different parts of your body—your arms, legs, head, and back. You can also move your whole body from one place to another. How do you do this? The answer lies under your skin!

Moving Part of Your Body

Under your skin are fat, soft muscles, and hard bones. The fat and muscles make a soft padding between your skin and some of your bones. Muscles make your bones move.

▲
You have two long bones in your lower arm and one long bone in your upper arm. Muscles move these bones to move your arm—to make it bend, straighten, and twist.

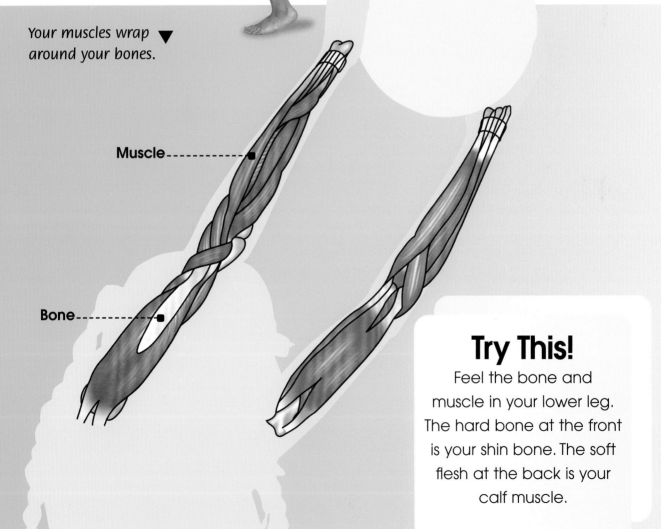

When you run, your ▶ muscles are working hard under your skin to help you take longer, faster steps.

Moving Your Whole Body
You move your feet and legs to get from place to place. Muscles work together to bend your knees and move the bones in your legs and feet.

Your muscles wrap ▼ around your bones.

Muscle- - - - - - - - - -■

Bone- - - - - - - - - -■

Try This!
Feel the bone and muscle in your lower leg. The hard bone at the front is your shin bone. The soft flesh at the back is your calf muscle.

Your Skeleton

Your skeleton is made up of all the bones in your body. Your skeleton is a framework inside your body that gives you your shape. Without bones, your body would be floppy.

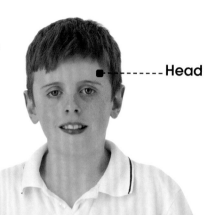

-------- Head

Arm

Each bone has its ▶ *own name. This is different from the name you give the outside part of the body. For example, the bone inside your head is called the skull.*

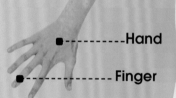

■---------- Hand

■----------- Finger

Bony Framework
When you were born, you had more than 350 different bones. As you grow up, some bones join together to make one bone. Adults have just 208 bones.

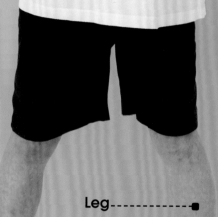

Leg------------■

Foot----

Strong and Rigid

Bones are hard and very strong. They do not break easily and they do not bend. You can't bend your lower arm because the bones inside are rigid.

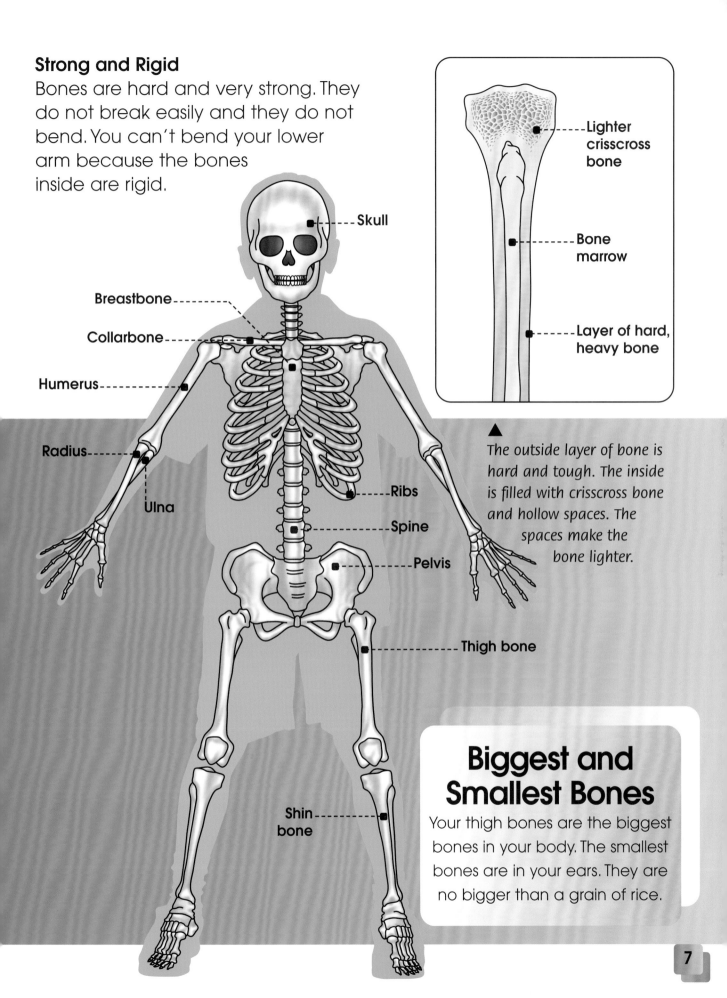

Skull

Breastbone

Collarbone

Humerus

Radius

Ulna

Ribs

Spine

Pelvis

Thigh bone

Shin bone

Lighter crisscross bone

Bone marrow

Layer of hard, heavy bone

▲

The outside layer of bone is hard and tough. The inside is filled with crisscross bone and hollow spaces. The spaces make the bone lighter.

Biggest and Smallest Bones

Your thigh bones are the biggest bones in your body. The smallest bones are in your ears. They are no bigger than a grain of rice.

Body Armor

Some bones protect important parts of your body called organs. These bones are like a suit of armor.

Bony Helmet

If you gently tap your head, you can feel your skull under the skin. This bone surrounds your brain—the organ that controls almost every part of your body.

Skull

Brain

Your skull is thick ▶ and extra strong. It has to be strong to protect your soft, squashy brain from being injured.

Rib Cage

Your ribs are curved, narrow bones. They protect two important organs—your heart and lungs. Your lungs take in air when you breathe in and your heart pumps blood around your body.

Under your chest, your ribs curve around from your spine to your breastbone. They form a rigid cage over your heart and lungs. ▼

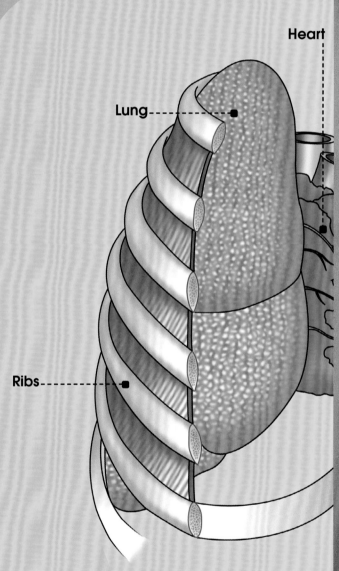

Heart

Lung----

Ribs-------

Try This!

Try to count how many ribs you have on each side of your body. You can feel your ribs on the side of your body, under your arms.

Joints

A joint is where two or more bones meet. Joints hold the ends of the bones together and allow them to move easily.

Moving Bones

You can only move your bones at your joints. You move your arms at your shoulders and elbows. You move your legs at your hips and knees.

Different joints allow you to ▶ move in different ways. Your shoulders let you move your arm in all directions, but at the knee, you can only swing your leg backward and forward.

Try This!

Try moving different joints in your body. How many ways does each one move?

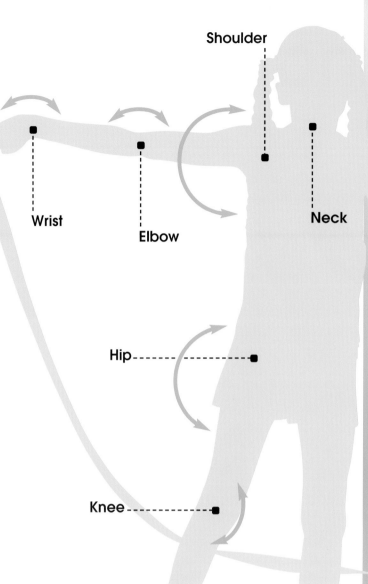

Shoulder

Wrist

Elbow

Neck

Hip

Knee

Ankle

▲
Joints have different names.
These are the main joints.

Ligaments are like straps. ▶
They hold the ends of the
bone together in the joint.

Inside a Joint

The ends of the bones are covered with soft cartilage. The cartilage stops the bones from rubbing together. Some joints, such as your knee, also contain liquid to help them move smoothly.

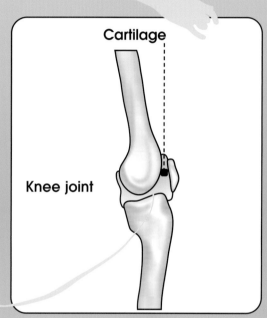

Cartilage

Knee joint

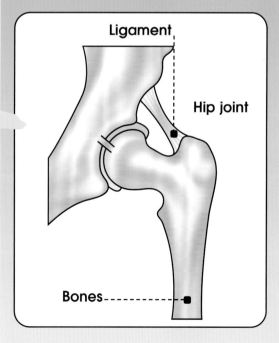

Ligament

Hip joint

Bones

Fingers and Thumbs

You use your hands to pick up and hold things such as pens, forks, and books. The joints in your fingers and thumbs allow you to do this.

Bending Your Fingers

The joints inside your fingers are hinge joints. They only let your fingers bend and straighten. They work like the hinges that join a door to the wall and let it open and close.

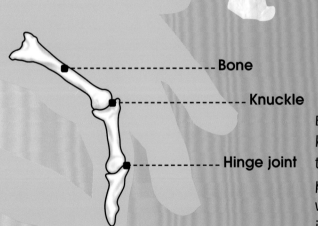

Bone - **Bone**

Knuckle - - - - - - - - - - - - - - - - - **Knuckle** ◀

Hinge joint - - - - - - - - - - - - - - **Hinge joint**

Each finger has two hinge joints that divide the finger into three parts. You move the whole finger using the joint inside your knuckle.

Moving Your Thumb

As well as bending and straightening your thumb, you can move it around in circles. This is because it is joined to your hand by a saddle joint. This allows a wide range of movements.

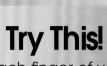

Try This!

Touch each finger of your hand with your thumb. Only humans, apes, and most monkeys can do this! This is because we have opposable thumbs. This special ability allows us to write and use other tools.

Saddle joint

You use your thumb and fingers to hold a pen or a paintbrush.
▼

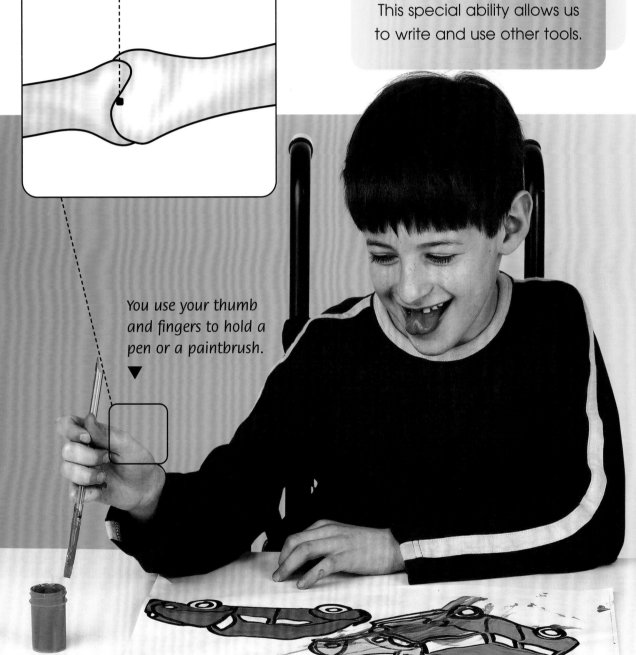

Shoulders and Hips

The joints inside your shoulders and hips give more movement than any other joint. They are called ball and socket joints.

The top of the thigh bone is shaped like a ball. It fits into a round space, called the socket, inside the hip.

▼

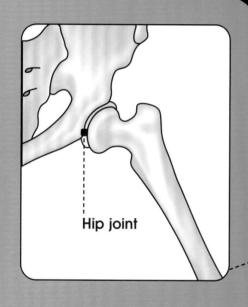

Hip joint

Moving Your Hips
Your leg moves from your hip. As you swing it forward or out in a circle, the top of the thigh bone moves around inside the hip joint.

Swinging Your Arms

You can reach out in almost every direction with your arms. But the joint inside your shoulder stops you from swinging your arms as far backward as you can forward.

Ligaments around each shoulder joint keep the top of your arm bone inside your shoulder joint. They stop your arm from slipping out.
▼

Doing the Splits

Some people can move their legs so far apart they can do the splits! This is because their hip joints can move farther than other people's.

Your Neck

The joint inside your neck allows you to nod your head and turn it from side to side. You can even see behind you just by twisting your head!

Moving Your Head

The joint inside your neck is a pivot joint. A round hole at the bottom of the skull fits over a spike at the top of the spine.

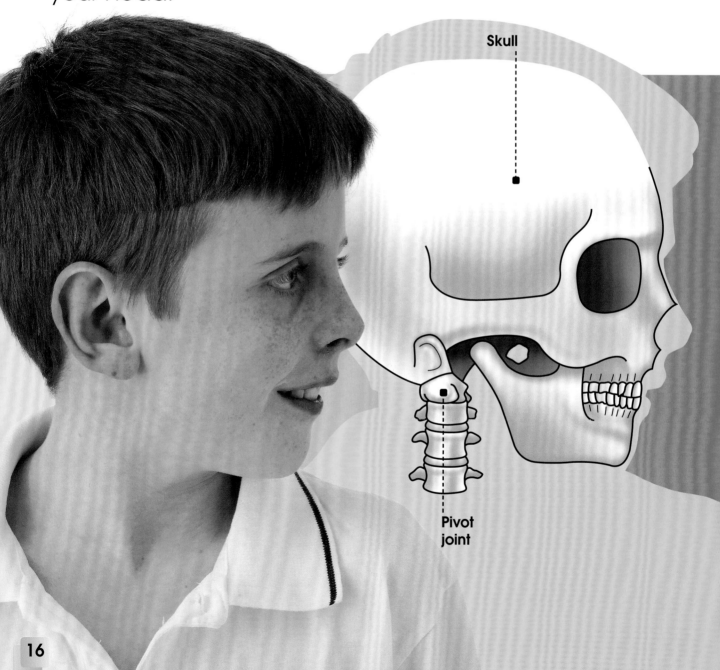

Skull

Pivot joint

Holding Up Your Head

Your neck not only lets you move your head, it also holds it in place. The spike inside the joint stops your head from slipping off your neck.

This girl's neck is so strong she can carry a heavy weight on her head. She balances it so that her skull is not tilted on her neck joint.
▼

◀ As you turn your head, your skull turns around the spike inside your neck joint. The bone around the pivot supports the skull and allows it to rock up and down so you can nod your head.

Try This!

Balance a book on your head. Make sure your head is perfectly straight. How far can you walk with it?

Your Spine

Your spine is an amazing column of knobbly bones that hold your body together. Your arms, legs, head, and all the bones in your trunk are attached to your spine.

Back Bones

The knobbly bones in your spine are called vertebrae. They fit into each other to make a strong column of bones.

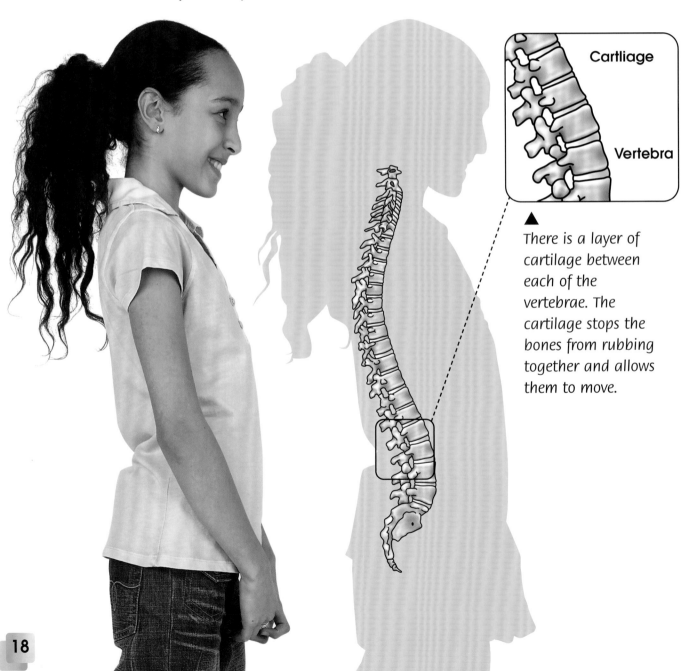

Cartliage

Vertebra

▲ There is a layer of cartilage between each of the vertebrae. The cartilage stops the bones from rubbing together and allows them to move.

Bending and Twisting

The vertebrae and cartilage allow you to bend and twist to one side or the other. If your spine had just one bone, you could not bend at all.

When you bend, the vertebrae  *inside your waist move a little, but they still stay fitted together.*

Try This!

Move your fingers up and down your spine. Can you feel the knobbly vertebrae? Feel the vertebrae at your waist move as you bend over and straighten up.

Muscles Move Your Bones

Most of your bones are covered by muscles. You have about 650 different muscles, which gives your body a soft, rounded shape. Muscles work by pulling your bones to move them.

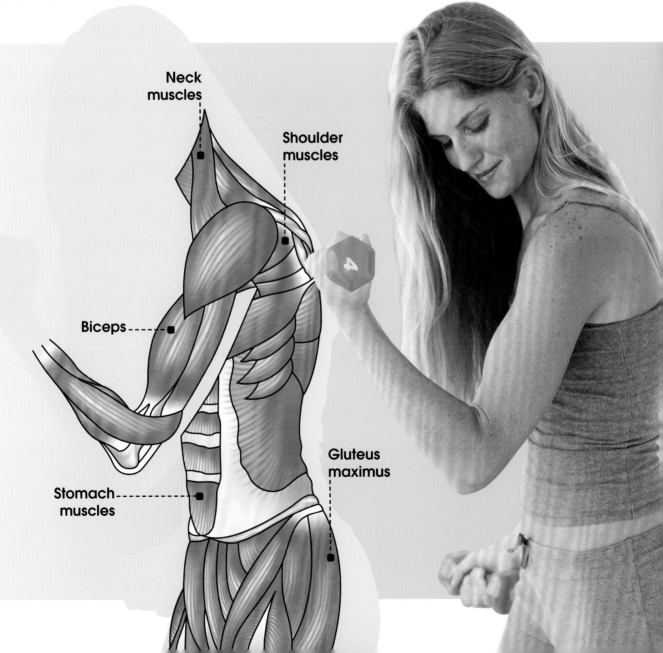

Neck muscles

Shoulder muscles

Biceps

Stomach muscles

Gluteus maximus

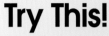

Try This!

Hold your calf and point your toes. Can you feel your calf muscle get tighter and harder?

Mapping the Muscles

Muscles pull your bones, but not the bones they cover. For example, your thigh muscle moves your lower leg.

How a Muscle Works

The muscles that move your foot are in your calf. They are attached to the bones in your foot by strong cords called tendons.

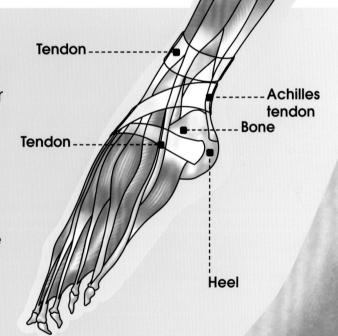

Calf muscle

Tendon

Tendon

Achilles tendon

Bone

Heel

When your calf muscles ▶ contract, the tendons pull your foot so it moves at the ankle joint. The main tendon is the Achilles tendon.

Moving Your Elbow

When a muscle contracts, it pulls a bone. Muscles only pull—they cannot push. This means that most muscles work in teams to pull a bone in different directions.

Bending Your Arm

The muscles that bend and straighten your lower arm are in your upper arm. The muscle that bends your arm is called the biceps.

Ulna

Biceps

Tendon

Elbow joint

▲
The tendon from the biceps is attached to the ulna, one of the bones inside the lower arm. When the biceps contracts, the tendon pulls up the lower arm.

Straightening Your Arm

A different muscle straightens your arm.
It is called the triceps and it is at the
back of your upper arm. When the
triceps contracts, the biceps relaxes.

Try This!

Hold your upper arm while
you bend and straighten
your arm. Can you feel the
biceps and triceps muscles
contracting and relaxing?

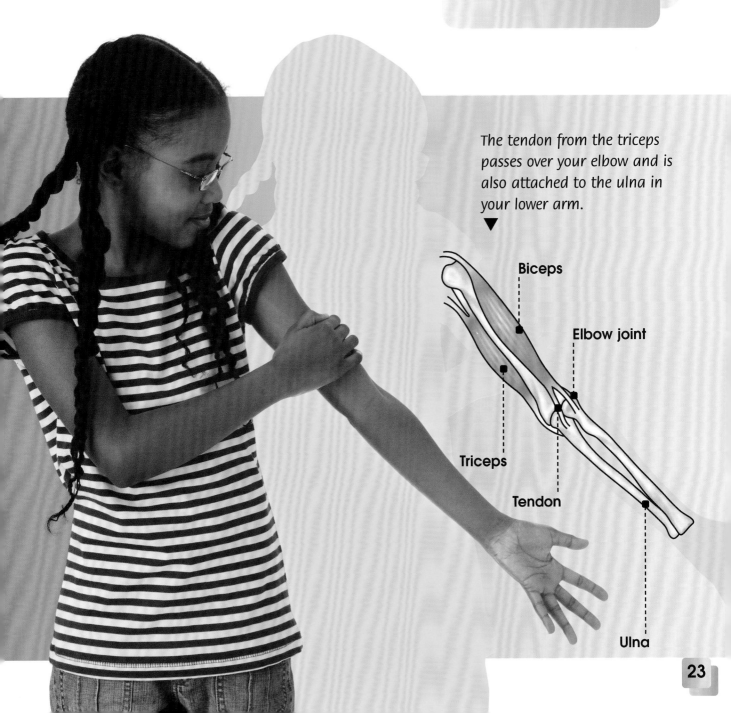

The tendon from the triceps
passes over your elbow and is
also attached to the ulna in
your lower arm.
▼

Biceps

Elbow joint

Triceps

Tendon

Ulna

Exercise

Exercise makes your muscles and joints become stronger. Most exercise uses many muscles working together. You are not usually aware which muscles you are using—you contract and relax them without thinking.

Swimming
Swimming exercises nearly all your muscles. The more you exercise, the better your muscles work and the longer you can keep going before you get tired.

You move your arms, legs, and head when you swim. This uses muscles in your stomach, chest, neck, and ◄ back as well as in your arms and legs.

Dancing
Dancing helps you to balance and exercises muscles in your stomach, arms, and legs. Dancing exercises your joints as well as your muscles.

Dancing helps your muscles ► and joints work better.

Biggest Muscles
The biggest muscles are the gluteus maximi in your buttock. You use them to stand up and to run. They also give you a soft cushion to sit on.

Moving Your Face

Not all your muscles move bones. The muscles in your face move your lips, cheeks, and brow. A tiny muscle opens your eyelids. You use it every time you blink!

Eating and Talking

The lower jaw is the only bone in your head that you can move. You move it to open and shut your mouth when you eat and when you talk.

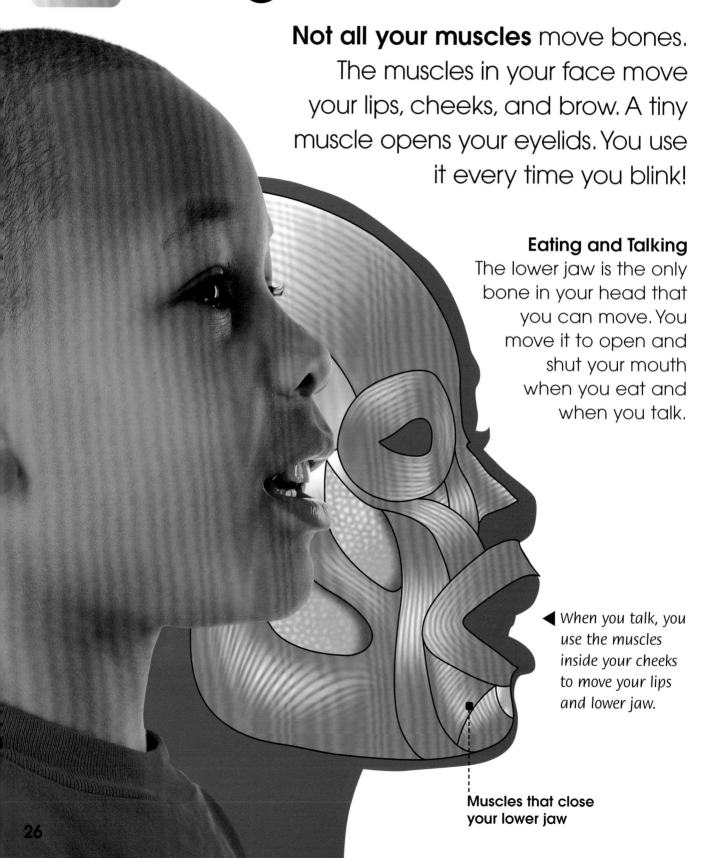

◀ When you talk, you use the muscles inside your cheeks to move your lips and lower jaw.

Muscles that close your lower jaw

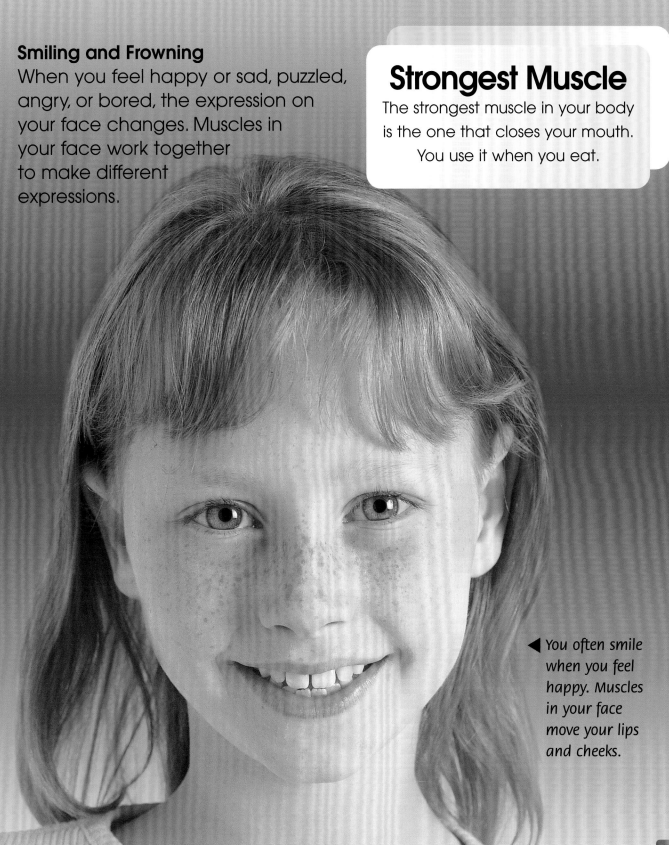

Smiling and Frowning

When you feel happy or sad, puzzled, angry, or bored, the expression on your face changes. Muscles in your face work together to make different expressions.

Strongest Muscle

The strongest muscle in your body is the one that closes your mouth. You use it when you eat.

◀ You often smile when you feel happy. Muscles in your face move your lips and cheeks.

Breaks and Sprains

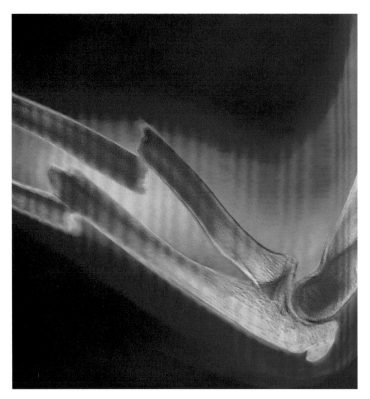

You may injure a bone or joint if you have a bad fall. You may break a bone, or you may sprain a joint. Breaks and sprains can take several weeks to heal.

◀ *The X-ray shows broken bones in an arm. A doctor straightens the broken bones and wraps a special bandage around the arm. New bone grows across the breaks to make the arm whole again.*

Broken Bone

A broken arm or leg is very painful. A doctor wraps a special bandage around the broken bone and joint. The bandage makes a hard cast that protects the bone while it heals.

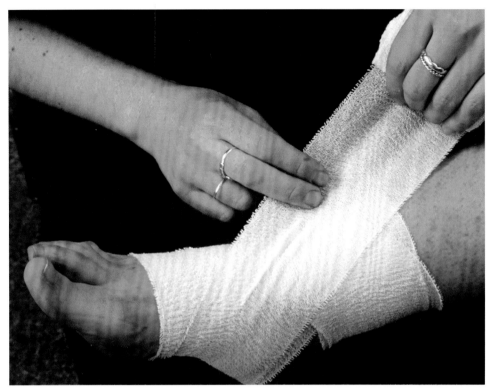

Sprained Ankle

A sprain happens when you tear a ligament around a joint. If you sprain your ankle, for example, the joint will swell up and be very painful.

◀ *A nurse wraps a stretchy bandage around the sprain. The bandage supports the ankle until it heals.*

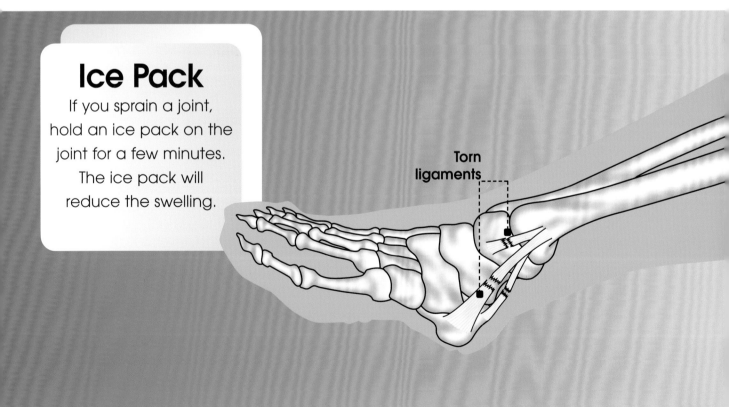

Ice Pack

If you sprain a joint, hold an ice pack on the joint for a few minutes. The ice pack will reduce the swelling.

Torn ligaments

Glossary

bone marrow
A fatty substance inside long bones.

bones
The hard parts of the body that lie under your skin and muscle.

brain
The organ that controls most of the things that happen in your body, including your thoughts and feelings.

cartilage
The soft, squashy material that is found at the ends of bones and in the flap of your ear.

cast
A hard shell in the shape of an arm or leg or other injured part of the body.

expression
The look on your face that shows what you are feeling or thinking.

gluteus maximus (plural glutei maximi)
The large muscle in the buttock.

heart
An organ made of a special kind of muscle. The heart pumps blood through your arteries to all parts of your body.

joint
The place where two or more bones meet and fit together.

knuckle
The joint in your hand where one end of your finger meets your hand. You can see your knuckles on the back of your hand.

ligament
The strap that holds the bones in a joint together.

lungs
The organs that take in air when you breathe in.

muscle
A fleshy tissue that is able to contract and relax to move a part of the body.

opposable thumb
A thumb that can touch each of the fingers on the same hand.

organ
A part of the body, such as the brain, heart, stomach, and lungs, that does a particular job.

rigid
Something is rigid when it is stiff and unbending.

tendon
The strong cord that joins a muscle to the bone it moves.

vertebra
One of the bones in your spine.

X-ray
A special kind of photograph that shows the bones inside your body.

Further information
WEB SITES
http://science.nationalgeographic .com/science/health-and-human-body/human-body/
This site allows you to select a part of the body and explore it.

www.kidshealth.org
This site gives you information about your body. Click on the section called "for kids."

Index